RAYMOND BRIGGS

Ethel & Ernest

ALFRED A. KNOPF

NEW YORK

1999

THIS IS A BORZOI BOOK
PUBLISHED BY ALFRED A. KNOPF, INC.

Copyright © 1998 by Raymond Briggs

All rights reserved under International and
Pan-American Copyright Conventions. Published in the
United States by Alfred A. Knopf, Inc., New York.
Distributed by Random House, Inc., New York.

www.randomhouse.com

Originally published in Great Britain by
Jonathan Cape, London, in 1998.

Knopf, Borzoi Books, and the colophon are registered
trademarks of Random House, Inc.

ISBN 0-375-40758-8

Manufactured in Singapore
First United States Edition

Ethel & Ernest

MONDAY 1928

TUESDAY

WEDNESDAY

4

ETHEL! FOR HEAVEN'S SAKE! WHERE **ARE** YOU?

Coming, Madam.

THURSDAY

ETHEL!

FRIDAY

SATURDAY

How about coming to the pictures with me?

Oooh...

5

Victor McLaglen!

Who's he?

Him up there.

Oh.

My favourite!

Oh.

Lovely flowers, darling.

Oh, that's Dad. He's potty about the garden.

Did you all grow up here?

Yes. Eleven of us. Thirteen with Mum and Dad. Bob, Beaty, Mag, Edie, me, Frank, Flo, Jessie, George, Joe and Bill.

George was killed in the war. Bob died as a baby. Beaty died at two and a half.

1930
~
1940

Fair bit of garden. More than down home.

I've always wanted my own bit of garden.

Ooh, look! An aeroplane!

Must get rid of this range. I want a modern gas cooker.

And this boiler came out of the ark.

We'll have a kitchen **AND** a scullery! A sitting-room **AND** a dining-room! A garden **AND** a shed! Don't forget the **HALL!** and the **BATHROOM!**

LUXURY!

HOORAY!

The Lovers' Seat

Fairlight Glen · Hastings · 1930

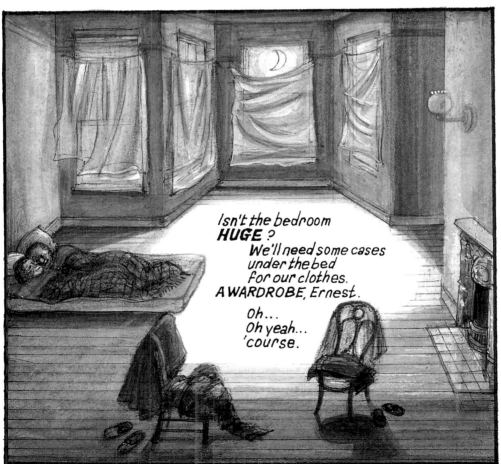

16

UGH! I hate coal under the stairs! Coal dust gets everywhere and—

It's SO **COMMON!**

I'll build a brick bunker in the garden...

That'll be lovely.

Smashing bed! Nearly new. Mahogany, I think... Good springs, look!

Newly-weds need good springs!

Come and try it out, darling...

Certainly **NOT**, Ernest! It's broad **DAYLIGHT!**

19

21

When was it? Hour ago. About five...

I was just doing Ashen Grove.
I nearly run out of Sterilised.
How do you feel?
You look done in. Tired...

It's all red. He...
It's a he...

Mr. Briggs, a word?

It was touch and go.

Oh?

Your wife is thirty-eight.

There had better not be any more.

More children... no more wife.

I'm sorry.

Good day to you.

But we wanted a proper family...

23

This gas copper is a real luxury!

Just turn the tap and strike a match!

The BBC's going to start "Tele-vision" later this year...

Oh? What's that when it's at home?

Well, it looks like a wireless set with pictures on top of it.

MOVING pictures? Talkies?

Yes. It'll be like going to the pictures without going out.

What? You'll just sit and look at it?

Yes.

I suppose it might be all right for the gentry.

It says "The average family needs £6 a week to keep it above the poverty line..."

What's the poverty line?

Dunno, I just wish I earned £6 a week.

27

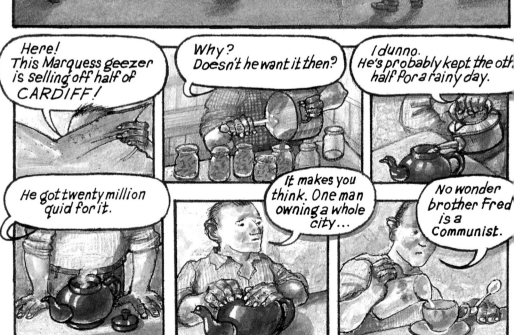

29

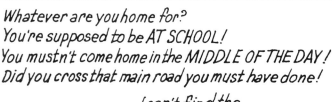

Whatever are you home for?
You're supposed to be AT SCHOOL!
You mustn't come home in the MIDDLE OF THE DAY!
Did you cross that main road you must have done!

I can't find the
sit down lavatories.
We SHOWED you them!
No. They're GIRLS.
Girls sit down.
NO! There's BOYS' sitting downs as well.

No there ISN'T!
It's all GIRLS.
Look out!
I want to go Number Twos.

Sounds like
that Hitler's
on the warpath
good and
proper.

Our George
was killed in
the last one.

And brother
Tom.

It doesn't seem
all that long ago.

Our poor old mother
never got over it.
She died at —

Mum!
What have I got to wear
red, white and blue
to school for?
        Because it's Empire Day.
What's empire?

Do keep
STILL!

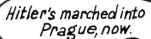

Hitler's marched into Prague, now.

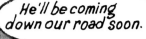

He'll be coming down our road soon.

Adolf Hitler in Wimbledon Park!

It's going to be very stuffy with all this blackout up, Ernest.

Not half as stuffy as a gas-proof room would be.
You have to bung up the chimney, tape over the cracks round doors and windows, put wet newspapers in between the floorboards...

It's a right old barney.

POISON GAS!

I hadn't thought of that.

♪ Underneath the spreading chestnut tree,
Mr. Chamberlain said to me, ♪
if you want your gas mask fitted free -
Join the blinking A.R.P. ♪

33

34

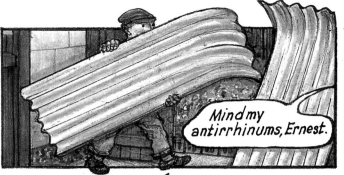

Mind my antirrhinums, Ernest.

I hope you know what you're doing.

Is that it finished?

That's it. All done!

Is it really bombproof?

We'll have to wait and see.

36

Russia's invaded Finland now.   I thought they'd invaded POLAND?

Yes, they have.   But you said GERMANY's invaded Poland?

Yes, that's right.   Well, who was it invaded Czechoslovakia?

Germany.   Germany's always invading someone.
I expect they'll invade Russia one day –

Cor blimey! Not likely!
They're IN LEAGUE!   or Russia will invade Germany.

Oh don't be DAFT!   If they ALL keep invading one another,
WE'LL end up invading someone.

Oh Et! You just don't
understand politics.

1940
~
1950

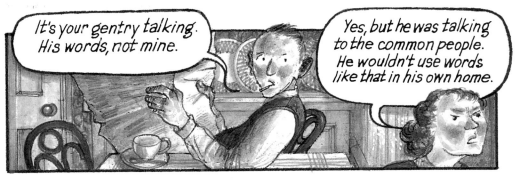

The battle for France is over...
the Battle of Britain is about to begin.
Upon this battle depends the survival
of Christian civilization.
The whole fury and might of the enemy
must, very soon, be turned on us.
Hitler knows that he will have to break us
in this island, or lose the war.

If we can stand up to him, all Europe
may be free and the life of the world
may move forward into broad sunlit uplands.

But, if we fail, the whole world
will sink into the abyss of a new dark age.
Let us, therefore, brace ourselves to our duty
and so bear ourselves that if the
British Empire last for a thousand years,
men will still say:

THIS was their finest hour.

Broad sunlit
uplands!

Good old Winston!
Our finest hour!

I expect Jerry will
be coming over soon.

They're starting to
take away our nice
gate and railings.

I'll make a
wooden gate.

Shame.

They want
saucepans, too.
They make them
into Spitfires.

Funny to think
of our front gate
being a Spitfire.

43

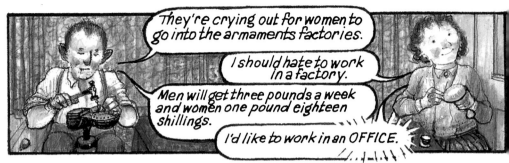

Look! It's come up!

What's that, son?

A pear tree! Auntie Flo gave me the pips from a pear we ate.

It had better not get too big, it'll block out all the light.

Don't discourage the boy, Ernest, I like a nice pear.

DARLING! **LABOUR'S WON!** WE'RE IN!

LABOUR WINS

Such a shame for poor Mr. Churchill.

The working man will be all right now. AT LAST!

He saved our bacon in the war.

Bloody MARVELLOUS!

ERNEST! Mr. Churchill never swears. He's a gentleman.

I'm Labour, Mum.

Sssh, dear.

56

57

58

59

1950
~
1960

Dad... Hullo.

Dad...

When you come
home from work... Yeah?

Why don't you wash
in the BATHROOM? Blimey son! Not likely! I'm filthy, look.

Yes, I know but that is
what the bathroom is FOR! No. Not in the BATHROOM.
Not in THIS state.

But this is the KITCHEN!
All the FOOD is in HERE!
Mum is trying to COOK! No. I couldn't, son.
Not in the BATHROOM.

That laundrette is a Godsend!
I did the whole blessed lot
for two and nine.
AND it's all bone DRY!

We could chuck out the mangle and the copper
I could get an electric thermostat for the tank
Hot water in the SUMMER time!

MODERN!

69

73

Dear, oh dear...
"BRITISH RAIL LOSES
SIXTEEN MILLION QUID"

It's Nationalised, isn't it?

'COURSE IT IS!

I thought so.

It says they're wanting to
legalise Homo-Sexuality.   Oh? What's that?

Well.. you know....it's like-
two BLOKES.
Only... instead of with a WOMAN,
sort of with-one another...like...

I don't know what
you're rambling on
about, Ernest, and I don't
think you do either.

I'll...er-put the kettle on,
shall I, duck?
Nice cup of tea?

75

We should have this HI-FI now, duck. Oh? What's that?

Well, it's sort of like having two wirelesses on at once. One for each ear. Extravagant.

It's a radiogram as well, though. Plays records. We haven't got any records.

No, but if we had, you could put them on and hear the STEREO. The what?

The STEREO. It comes out in STEREO. What does?

The music from the HI-FI. It's "PAN-OR-AM-IC SOUND" it says. 3D. Three dee?

Yeah, 3D, 'course. I don't think I want to bother with it.

Here! This soppy bishop says: 'Mothers who work full-time are the enemies of family life."

It's all right for *HIM*, living in a *PALACE* with *SERVANTS!*

He was brought up to different standards, Ernest. He's a GENTLEMAN Christian.

Here Et, listen. It says we've got to be **HIP**.

What?

GROOVY, babe. And **REAL COOL**.

Just talk sense, Ernest.

We've got to **HANG LOOSE** with the **CATS**.

Cats?

YEAH, MAN!

Ernest! Go to bed.
You're overtired.
I'll make the cocoa.

You're a **SQUARE**, baby.

Oh, Ernest...
When will you grow up?

1960
~
1970

That green car! | Well?
Triumph Herald! | What about it?
Wasn't there yesterday. | There's always different cars stuck outside our house nowadays.

That one's special. | What's special about it?

It's **OURS!**

Oh don't be daft, Ernest.

Come on, dear. Get in. | Ooh - er...
I don't like to...
I've still got my pinny on.

I haven't done my hair.

Is it really yours?

OURS, darling.

I didn't know you could drive a proper car.

81

When are you going to start a family, dear?

Well... don't know really, Mum. Probably not at all.

Goodness me! Why ever not? I want to be a granny.

Well, Jean's got problems, Mum. Brain trouble.

BRAIN TROUBLE!

Yeah...well...that's just what I call it - as a sort of...joke... She goes in and out of the loony bin.

You mean...she's - mental?

Yeah. That's one word for it. The other word is - Schizophrenia.

Oh, dear! Poor thing!

So I won't be a granny after all?

Never mind, Mum.

What a dump.

DUMP! MUM! The Government has designated this an **AONB**. An **A**rea of **O**utstanding **N**atural **B**eauty! It's **OFFICIAL!**

I still say it's a dump.

The South Downs are at the end of the garden!

I give up... I give up...

Son... It's the sort of place I've always dreamed about.

86

87

MAN ON THE MOON, Eh!

FANTASTIC, eh? *Oh?*

What's he doing there?

Well, just walking about a bit.

Then what?

Well...come back, I suppose...

Perhaps they'll have a picnic.

That would be nice.

I think the tea would blow away
when it came out of the thermos.

Why? Is it windy up there?

No, it's gravity, dear.

Oh, I see.

Look! He's going to pick up
some pebbles...to take home.

Just like kiddies at the seaside.

Turn it off, will you?

88

1970
~
1971

Decimal Currency starts next week!

Oh yes, I've heard about it on the television.

It's dead simple! See – a bob equals **FIVE** New Pence. Two bob is **TEN** New Pence.

What's a ha'penny?

There isn't one – oh yes, there is! Half a New Pence – looks like a farthing.

What about threepenny bits?

Gone, duck. A tanner is two and a half New Pence.

And what about half a crown?

Er...well...that'll be – two bob equals ten New Pence, a tanner equals two and a half New Pence, so ten plus two and a half is...twelve and a half New Pence. Easy!

What's a penny?

An **OLD** penny...well...a shilling is five New Pence, so twelve old pennies equals five **NEW** Pence, so **ONE** old penny is...twelve into five – Um...

How many shillings are there in the pound now?

Did you have a good journey, dear?

Oh yes, OK Mum. Fine. Fine.

Much traffic on the road?

Well, the A23 was a bit choked up, but after Sutton it sort of thinned out a bit...and... it got better...less traffic...um...

Here's a comb, dear.
Thanks, Mum.

Remember we used to bring the pram up here?

It's me in the pram, now.
They used to do nice teas in the balcony before the war.
Waitresses in aprons and caps...

We never did go, did we, dear?

Yes.
It was lovely.

The yobboes smashed all the windows.

That's your Labour Party for you.

91

93

94